SO PEOPLE SAY YOU'RE AN ASSHOLE
A BOOK FOR YOU, PEOPLE WHO LOVE YOU, AND PEOPLE WHO WORK WITH YOU

SARAH BRABBS

COUNTRY SUN PRESS

So People Say You're An Asshole: A Book for You, People
Who Love You, and People Who Work with You
Country Sun Press
All Rights Reserved
ISBN 978-0-9972411-1-2

Ordering information: signed copy direct from author via
assholestore.com & available on Amazon.

Author information: optimizingrelationships.com

Cover Design © 2016 Jessica Angerstein
Editing by Lori Byron

This book is dedicated to the amazing people in my writing group. Thank you for being there throughout this whole process.

Table of Contents

Introduction and Should You Read This?

Welcome to my no fluff, take action book about assholes.

You should read this if you're an asshole, or if people think you're an asshole (but you don't agree...or maybe you do). You should also read this if you deal with an asshole frequently.

You should not read this if you are an asshole who enjoys being one or aren't interested in learning something new. It would be a waste of time for you.

My intention with this book is to make it a quick read that educates, impacts, and equips you to understand and deal with yourself and those in your life better than you do now. You should take whatever you learn that fits your life experience and run with it. That is, if you want to enjoy life and relationships more than you do right now.

And here's some advice from a teacher: if you want to remember this when you're done reading it, tell someone else who needs to know. Teaching is the best way to learn and retain information. But don't teach it to someone who doesn't want to know – otherwise you're the asshole.

This book is broken into three parts: The first part is So, People Say You're An Asshole, the second Assholes in Relationships, and finally Assholes at Work. You can skip sections if you wish, but I encourage you to read this start to finish.

Also I should mention: often when we think of the word "asshole" we automatically apply that label to a male, but this term applies to women, as well. I most frequently refer to males here when I talk about assholes for the sake of simplicity, but know that it can refer to men or women. In fact, two females who have been assholes to people I love were my inspiration to write this book.

This is not a long book. That is because I am someone who values succinct communication and straight talk. I want you to quickly read this, get it, apply it, and move on with your life.

I've been told before I have the gift of delivering truths with a "velvet brick" style, meaning I can deliver hard truths but be nice in the process, and people are able to "hear" these hard truths from me. I hope that you have a velvet brick experience.

One last thing: you will see the word asshole fairly often as you read. Believe it or not, I don't swear a lot in my life. There's just no better word for what I'm writing about than asshole, so it's frequently necessary.

Part 1 - So, People Say You're an Asshole

If you're an asshole and not completely unaware of yourself, usually you know you are one.
But...let me paint a picture of what your life is like at times. See if you recognize yourself.

- When you get in arguments with people you feel like an innocent victim
- You usually think the problem is someone else
- You express the above in a variety of ways – often not very nicely
- You don't make it a habit to think about the effect you have on others
- You notice people don't often seek out your company
- You are called an asshole

The good news is that if any of this resonates with you, you know where you are now, and awareness is always the first step. So, yes, you can be an asshole. There's nuance in this label, though, and this is important to understand. There's a difference between behavior - *you can be* asshole – and identity - *you are* an asshole. One of the meanest labels to assign someone is that of an asshole. It's also ironic if you think about it because calling someone an asshole could be described as an asshole move.

This label gets applied to you *over time* as people experience communication and behaviors from you – the asshole label allows for them to make sense of it all. Sure, the person assigning that label may not be innocent either...but more on that later.

What's True is Not the Whole Truth

You CAN BE an asshole is the truth. You ARE an asshole really isn't the whole truth. I use can and are interchangeably, but realize that no one always IS an asshole. This implies that 100% of the time, you are an asshole. But really, people are assholes just some of the time. We all have good days, right? If you are constantly told you're an asshole that just means you've graduated to the "always an asshole" label *in someone else's mind*. Therefore you've been assigned this very negative character trait for the foreseeable future.

The truth is most of us can be mean, defensive, argumentative, and downright nasty at times or in certain circumstances. So, imagine "being an asshole" as a continuum. Most people fall on this scale somewhere, whether it's at the low end, Not Often (a 1 or 2) - or towards the high end, Nearly Always (9 or 10). Hopefully at the end of this book you'll find yourself at a lower number than when you started.

When you are on the high side of the continuum and your behavior is affecting *you* negatively, (which might be the reason you are reading this book) is when you experience the results of your behavior. Cause and effect.

The Consequences of Asshole Behavior

Some of the effects or consequences to asshole behavior are: You cannot be consistently kind, so lovers leave you at some point. Or the two of you get stuck in a very unhealthy, yet addictive cycle, so she/he hasn't left you...yet.

At work, people may disrespect or fear you (depending on your position), and most don't like you. You may not keep friends for long, unless they are at arm's length, or they are assholes too. Often you won't have any close friends. Your family knows you can be an asshole, but if you're lucky, they love you, anyway. If you're not lucky, you've probably alienated them too. Or worse, your family could be one of the catalysts for your asshole behavior.

Your Family

Being an asshole as an adult brings up the old nature versus nurture debate, which is worth touching on briefly. Your family of origin is your first communication and behavior "classroom." They are who you learn all your behaviors from, even before you get out into the world in school and begin interacting with others. If your mom flies off the handle at nothing and tries to control everything, you could take after her. This kind of short fuse and control issue makes for an easy slide into asshole-dom. Your mom, for instance, may have been the first asshole you experienced and learned from.

If your dad models silence as a method of communication in arguing, you will grow up thinking it is normal to display silence in the face of an angry partner.

On the other hand, you may have had a perfectly positive family experience and still turned out to be someone others describe as an asshole – that's where nature comes in. We all have certain personality traits that are stable over time. We may be uptight, laid back, outgoing, introverted, talkative, etc.

But for now, let's move on to those of you who would say you "know" you ARE an asshole, or even before reading the above, would've said unequivocally that you are an asshole.

The truth is, you belong in the first category, too. You *can be* an asshole. At some point in your life you were not an asshole (even if you have to go back to your toddler years). You have days when you are nice, not an asshole. But we all have the capability to be an asshole.

If you "can be" an asshole, if follows that you also "can *not be*" an asshole.

This book is for you if you want different results in your life than you're currently getting. To do this successfully, you will need to get over and see past yourself.

You are not going to learn what you need to know on your own or you wouldn't be where you are today.

Why You're an Asshole

Before we look at things to do differently at home and work, it's helpful to examine why you tend to act like an asshole. Being an asshole translates to not demonstrating respect for another person. You think less of them for some reason. You're probably already on track to understand and change this because you're reading this book. Someone who has decided they'll be this way forever has no interest in learning how to change.

In general, people around you are worthy of your respect simply because they're the same as you – a walking, talking, breathing human being. They may be less one thing, and more another thing, they may believe different things about life than you do, have a different cultural background for instance, but they are just as much a person as you are. And who they are is directly the result of what their life has been like until now, just like you.

We also have much to learn from others if we are open to it, but this requires that we respect others and have some humility.

If humility doesn't come naturally to you, intentionally opening your mind and life experience to be more humble will feel strange at first, but don't worry. Here in this moment reading this book, no one will know how you're feeling except you! And it'll be worth it.

But I'm Not Good at Dealing with People

We hear a lot these days about using our strengths. We're told to focus on what we're good at and we'll be more satisfied and successful in life. Of course this is true.

But it doesn't get us off the hook when it comes to looking at things we need to change that are within our power to change. Being an asshole is one of those things, and not being an asshole involves learning to deal differently with people around you. Deciding you "just can't deal with people" because you are (fill in the blank) is just something you tell yourself.

But really this is a limiting way of thinking, one that if you keep believing, means you won't ever give yourself the chance to change. It's like a child deciding they can't cook when they've hardly tried. This child then becomes an adult who eats out for every meal, or makes macaroni and cheese at home.

I mentioned earlier that we have certain personality traits that are stable over time. These are things like shyness, being easygoing, excitability, etc. Those traits don't change much. But along the way, we may decide that something is a part of our core identity. We then hold onto it for all it's worth, often not even realizing that we could be different. Let me give you a personal example.

We Create Our Identities

Fifteen years ago when I first studied communication, I did an exercise. In the exercise, I was instructed to write down things that I believed were core to my identity – "who I am." Things like, "I am funny," "I am organized" and so on. After I wrote down my core identity statements, I had to pick the ten most important, and then put my top ten in order of most important – or most *me*. When I did that, my second most important aspect to my identity was "I often say inappropriate things." What?!

The last part of the exercise involved mentally stripping away each one of these identifiers, one at a time, starting from the least important and ending with the most important, and stopping to "feel" what it felt like to lose each aspect of my identity.

It wasn't until I closely examined that belief about myself that I realized this actually wasn't true. The realization was so jarring at the time that I felt like I'd lost my balance. I had this strange, free-falling feeling in my stomach. I felt "off," but in a good way, even though it was a little scary. But this was an example of a thought that up until that moment, I *believed* and it was really limiting me. In the space of sixty seconds, I examined it and promptly discarded it as false.

But I thought about that belief. And I knew why I believed that. I grew up in a community of families who belonged to a strict religious group (nothing scary, just fairly conservative.) My family did everything we could to fit in and meet the norms of this group of people. And in the late 1970's and 80's, that meant kids were seen and not heard. Girls weren't to hang out with boys alone, and kids shouldn't talk too much, especially out of turn.

This meant that I received a lot of messages, both overtly and subtly, of disapproval when I spoke. And I was a kid who had a lot to say. Like many of us as children, I didn't have much self-awareness about how I communicated and what was wrong or what was okay. By being part of this group and experiencing the disapproval, I grew up with a belief that I tended to communicate inappropriately. And because I believed that, I did actually say strange things at times (none of which were *that* weird) but still, I believed that about myself, which meant I actually lived up to it.

The takeaway here is what we believe, the identifiers we hold about ourselves to be true or "the way I am," can really, really drive our experience of ourselves, our world, and ultimately, others' perception and experience of us.

13

So if you decide you are always right, or are stubborn, or are an asshole, or that no one will ever understand you...that will happen for you. But the one who will suffer most for being stuck the way you are is you.

In reality, if all of us were to slow down and take the time to think honestly about ourselves and to list our "identifiers," we'd see some truths, too.

For one thing, when we are really rude or mean to others, often what we actually are feeling is the loss of control, or threatened in some way. And neither of these are comfortable ways to feel.

Facts of (Adult) Asshole Life

In general, we like things our way. That means we know what we want, we don't want to be annoyed, and we expect certain things to be "just so" around us. The older we get, the more strongly we feel these preferences for certain things.

When we meet the inevitable acquaintance, friend, lover, or coworker who pushes our buttons it's annoying. And if it's someone close to us who really gets in our face, then our very identity feels threatened. It's easier to drive people away. Because when someone tries to do things their way or brings the full weight of who they are onto us (especially if we clash), then we feel a loss of control. Or at the very least, a vague feeling of discomfort that we'd prefer to distance ourselves from.

And, of course, as human beings we don't enjoy pain, so we don't want to deal with these feelings. If we mentally dwell on discomforts, we may feel anger, a sense of loss, or an out of control feeling.

So a cycle ensues. When we feel these ways, we enact communicative behaviors that have become etched into the fabric of our being as we've learned and perfected them over years.

In the moment, this can look like a quick temper, angry words, bad decisions, and fractured relationships. It means hurting the people we love, and then feeling terrible later (if we are aware of ourselves and reflect on the consequences of our behaviors.)

This situation is like a ball of rubber bands. Imagine the rubber bands in the ball are each made of confusing thoughts, reactions, unexamined assumptions, learned and practiced behavior, instinctual communication, and uncomfortable feelings. Rather than take apart our rubber band ball, we just toss it and it bounces with the same result every time: no progress, and often, we lose it.

In this book, the rubber band ball will get untangled.

Realize too that it's not just about your rubber band ball. We are surrounded by people every day who have their own messy ball.

It's amazing how many people out in the world act like assholes when there is a much better way to be, and life is so much more enjoyable when we aren't assholes. People like and respect us. We get promotions. We effectively manage those under us and relate respectfully to our coworkers, peers, and family. Our partners continue caring. Our kids don't ignore or hate us. Ultimately, instead of a negative impact, we have a positive impact on ourselves and our corner of the world.

About Me

Now is a good time to tell you about me. While I don't claim to have all the answers, what I know comes from my life, my training, and my gift of understanding people and how they communicate, especially assholes.

My entire adult life, I've been the one that people come to when they need help communicating and understanding others – in particular, difficult people. You would think I would've become a counselor, but I didn't.

Depending on who you ask, I'm a trainer, a writer, a coach, a teacher, or an inspirer.

I've made a study of communication, both throughout my life and inside higher education – first as a student, now as a college instructor. I also have a business in which I help others through communication workshops and trainings, speaking engagements, and coaching. Beyond my Master's Degree in Communication, I've also received Educator training at The Gottman Institute in Seattle, Washington.

Doctors John and Julie Gottman, psychologists who founded The Gottman Institute, have been researching what breaks and makes relationships work for over 40 years. They've followed over four thousand couples throughout their relationships and major life changes. They've studied families. And most important, they can predict divorce happening within five years with over 90% success rate after listening to a couple argue for five minutes. I'd highly recommend Dr. Gottman's book, "The 7 Principles to Making Marriage Work" if you are interested in this topic. A lot of what they teach can be extrapolated to any relationship.

I remember many years ago as I sat in various classrooms while pursuing my Master's Degree in Communication. At the school I attended, we mostly read studies and books, wrote papers, and talked about all kinds of communication. I vividly remember how I felt then - so frustrated because the people in my classes were NOT the ones who needed to learn this information.

The people who need to learn more about effective communication aren't typically getting advanced degrees in communication. They are out in the world, unaware that there's more to communication than meets the eye. It is that desire to reach the people who would never normally sit around and talk about communication that drove me to start my business and to write this book.

Of course, full disclosure: I also used to be an asshole sometimes. Don't get me wrong, I was usually nice and people liked me, but I was kind of an asshole, too. Before the age of 19 I was extremely self-centered, disrespectful to some people, and I thought I was the most important person in the world. It was all about my feelings, me, and my world. It doesn't feel amazing to admit this. But it's true.

Fortunately, I had some timely wake-up

conversations with people around me at the right time (velvet brickers, as described in the introduction.) I grew like a little weed after those; matured, and studied and matured, and studied. Ironically, the way I used to be laid the foundation for what I would spend my life doing: helping people communicate.

More about me later. Back to you.

Who You Are and Who You Can Be

To have any hope of changing your asshole behavior, you must first accept that you either are an asshole sometimes or you are perceived as an asshole (both have the same result) *and* that you have much to learn.

Also, try on these beliefs: It is possible for me not to be an asshole. It's possible to be happier than I am.

They are true. Best of all real change is not only possible, it's inevitable.

Why We Don't Think About Communication and Why It Matters

Most of us think we are great, or at least decent, at communicating, because we have been doing it our whole lives. We don't have to "think" to communicate.

But imagine that our communication endeavors are like swimming in a lake. Some of us are strong swimmers. We cut through the water to the other side with no difficulty and have a great time.

Some of us tread water and remain stuck the way we have always been, unaware that we could have a much better experience.

Some of us realize we could be a better swimmer, so we take lessons.

Some of us only know one type of stroke and don't care. We may tire quickly and have to rest frequently, but that's good enough.

Some drown. Some flail and grab onto others for support, almost drowning them in the process.

And finally... some don't even know there is a lake.

Living our lives, communicating with others, and behaving the way we do all happens in this "lake." Everything we do and say – or don't do and don't say - causes a ripple effect.

People who are drowning won't make it and often pull down others who try to help, the same way that people who are drowning pull down their rescuers. People who have left you may have experienced this. They've tried to help and when they were unsuccessful they disengaged, because it was the only way they would survive and thrive.

So here you are.

I'm Not Sure I Want to Keep Reading

Some of you may be tempted to stop reading this because as truth starts to penetrate, it isn't exactly a warm pleasant feeling. However, if you have a feeling of vague discomfort (but you're still drawn to read this), know this feeling is a good sign. It means what I'm saying is resonating with you. I believe if you are reading this book, there's a reason. There's something you have to learn.

This all may sit strangely with you because you're in uncharted territory, but trust me, it's good. Don't let any discomfort you feel get in the way.

Part 2 – Assholes and Relationships

What We Believe About Ourselves and Those Around Us Matters: You & Your Lover

It's important to touch on our beliefs again because what we believe about ourselves and others dictates how we respond to people, situations, and life in general.

For instance, think about the last time you were accused of being something that you are not. Let's take selfish – a really common one. Say you forgot to do something. You had a crazy day at work, didn't sleep much the night before, and you're affected by these two things on your way home. So you forget to stop for milk again, and this is the second time this week you've forgotten. For this, you're called selfish when you walk in the door. You are met with demands, lack of understanding, and critical messages from your other half.

"Why are you so forgetful? You're so wrapped up in yourself! You're so selfish." If the last accusation isn't made outright, it's certainly implied. (These things say as much about the person who says them than you, by the way.) That person, over time and through different experiences, has decided you're selfish, partially because you can't remember to do some things sometimes.

But if this person loves you *and* chooses to act out of that love and positive perception of you, then she knows you aren't inherently selfish. If she is aware enough of herself and her communication, she may instead greet you with, "Tough day? I noticed you forgot the milk again."

That way of approaching you is much friendlier and also more likely to create good results. It's very different from assuming the worst about you and acting from that perception. After all, just like you *can be* an asshole, so can your lover.

Realize that *what we believe about people and ourselves dictates how we treat others* and in turn, how they treat us. If someone believes the best of you it will show in how they communicate with you.

But if they are either an asshole themselves or they are sick of dealing with you (having had bad experiences), they will instead act out of the belief that you are ----- (fill in the blank with whatever negative characteristic you might have temporarily displayed.) And we know from experience that being treated as though you *are* something, based on one or two incidents, only builds on the relational troubles we already have.

In a relationship, it's more important to consider things like the above because over time, if you're treated this way or you treat your lover this way, at least one of you begins to feel that the other is no longer your friend. And ultimately, you act out of that belief.

It's the same if the roles are reversed.

If you snap at your partner when she asks how a home project is coming along, you may unintentionally convey to her the following:

- *You're annoying, stop hassling me*
- *You remind me of my mother, stop nagging me*
- *Stop interrupting me (you're not important enough)*
- *I don't respect you enough to respond*
- *You don't trust me*

Sure, you might just be tired. And if your partner isn't at the end of her rope and realizes you may have just had a tough day, she'll write it off as that. But if you snap at her routinely, it becomes an issue.

And if she's started to believe you are selfish or that your friendship as a couple is weakening (meaning she won't feel supported, understood, or respected), then this becomes simply another nail in that coffin of negative perception.

What she may have intended by asking is first, simple curiosity, nothing more. Or maybe, she is wondering where you're at on the project because other things depend on it. It probably does affect her, or she wouldn't be asking. She may be asking to remind you that the project is not completed – and why is this not okay?

Or she may be asking simply because she cares about you and what you're working on.

What significant others do *not* want is to be cast as the "nagger." They don't wish to be labeled with your mother's voice. They also (usually) are not implying a lack of trust or anything else negative. They are just asking. And they deserve a nice answer, not an asshole response.

It's up to you as the person who gets asked

"annoying" questions like these to take a breath and *think* before you respond. Remember: your partner is your equal. So respond with respect.

Of course, if she *constantly* asks you (also known as nagging) about things, she may need to be gently reminded that you are equals, you two go about completing tasks differently, and repeatedly asking won't make you want to do anything faster.

The above two scenarios highlight the ways our perceptions of people can change over time; the ways our beliefs and thoughts impact our communication; and how easy it can be to slide into trouble in our relationships.

One last thing before we move on - you'll notice that I frequently mention being friends inside of your romantic relationship. That is because at the core of your relationship, what you have is a very strong friendship. Your friendship is characterized as more because of your romantic feelings and commitment to one another, but beneath all of that is a true friendship. And the strength and quality of your friendship inside your relationship determines how long you'll stay together. More on this later.

Examining What is Actually True

When we examine what we believe to be true about our life, our thoughts, and the people around us it can be illuminating. Think about this for a minute.

- Do you trust that your partner wants what's best for you? For your family?
- Do you trust your partner is doing the best she can?
- Do you believe in your partner?

Now, what do you think she would say in response to these questions?

What would you want her to answer?

If you say yes, "I truly believe the best about my partner"...and then after some reflection you realize you don't demonstrate this consistently, then you need to review your actions and thoughts more closely.

Action Step One

Spend some time thinking about the above questions, and any other related questions that come to your mind. Taking the time to go through this exercise matters. Research shows that, over time if a couple habitually practices negative mindsets towards each other, they *don't even see half* of the positive things their partner does. It's as if 50% of those positive things simply didn't happen.

All of us have had the experience of doing something nice or saying something thoughtful, only to have our lover not notice or remember. In those moments, we feel like we're not truly "seen" and understood by our partner. This negative mindset can be the reason our good deeds go unnoticed. We see what we look for and expect.

Handling Anger in a Smart Way

When we're mad, we tend to think about all the reasons we are justified in our anger, and in the heat of those moments it is impossible to reason with us. So, if you're REALLY mad, know that nothing will hold your attention, apart from what is consuming you.

You can thank your fight-or-flight system for this. In these moments, your blood pressure has risen, your heart is racing, and it is physiologically impossible to think straight. In prehistoric times when our very survival was determined by our ability to outrun danger, we would be grateful for this.

But in the course of a normal fight it's detrimental - if we allow it to be. So when you're experiencing these physical reactions, the only positive thing to do in that moment is to take a break and come back to whatever is happening when you're completely calmed down. Only then will you think clearly.

The Importance of Apologizing and Letting Go

We can all be mean and say or do things we later regret. There's a term for this – amygdala hijack. This is when the emotion center of our brain is so tripped up, we lose control and act out of the fear or anger we feel in the moment. Daniel Goleman, an emotional intelligence guru, has written a lot about this. Again, the key is to allow yourself time to calm down. And if you did say or do something that later you regret, apologize. Not a fake apology ("I'm sorry you were so offended") but truly apologize and take responsibility.

But your saying sorry is just half of what needs to happen in a healthy relationship.

Your partner needs to practice letting it go and accepting your apology. The Gottmans have found this to be one of the keys to a successful relationship: whether the partner receives (or refuses) the apology, or in Gottman terms, a repair attempt (there's more to repair attempts - I'd recommend reading his book I mentioned earlier for more information or doing a search online.)

Just imagine trying to have a relationship with someone who never forgives you, never gives you another chance, and stacks all the wrongs you've done. The future you want with that person is not going to happen; unless you don't mind spending your time with someone who believes you don't live up to his or her standards and keeps track of your failings.

Assholes and Stress - Asshole-in-Recovery

When assholes get stressed, they become even more of an asshole. So when you, the asshole-in-recovery, are stressed, first realize you are stressed and think about why.

You may be stressed out for very good reasons. It's normal to be stressed at times in life.

What is not normal is to take it out on those around you, especially your partner. Did you know that one of the most important benefits to being in a long-term committed relationship is lower stress levels? One reason is that when we have someone to unburden ourselves to, who accepts us as we are, we actually feel better. Think about times of stress. Do you see your partner as your understanding ally, or as someone you want to hide your stress from, or someone you want to let have it? Which is it?

You want to get to the point where your partner is your ally. But to make that happen you have to trust her and confide in her. And most importantly when she confides in you, 99% of the time, she just needs you to listen, not fix her issues.

If she feels safe confiding in you and that you understand her (you don't need to agree to understand), she will give the same understanding back to you.

If the two of you can practice simply listening to each other during times of stress, and refrain from blaming, pointing out faults, shouting, and being assholes to each other you can actually make the normal stresses of life part of the strong bedrock in your relationship that keeps you close.

Sex: Powerful Relationship Glue

With stress, fights, and assholes in relationships, one of the casualties is often sex. I hear these phrases from clients, "we haven't had sex in a few months" or "gosh it's been…a year or two" (insert uncomfortable laugh.) Sex is hard to enjoy regularly if one of you is being an asshole. (Of course there are many other reasons sex is hard to make a regular event.) Practicing supporting each other and being each other's friend are key to help make sex and intimacy more frequent in your relationship.

Sex (unless you have had traumatic experiences) does so many good things for the two of you.

Obviously it feels good, but there's more. When you have sex, your bodies release hormones that bind you together on a cellular level. You feel closer emotionally as well as in ways that you don't have words for. You just find yourself feeling more drawn to your partner. The latter effect is partially physiological in nature. For one thing, our bodies release oxytocin to our brains – the cuddle hormone.

It's also hard to stay mad at someone you have sex with. Your attitude toward that person tends to be more favorable, just because you are physically intimate.

Sex is like the protective glue that keeps us together through many seasons of life; sex binds us. We are at our most physically vulnerable during sex, which often increases feelings of tenderness and commitment. So start planning to include more sex in your relationship.

You Have Young Children & Other Reasons

It can be hard for new parents to have regular sex. And full disclosure, I have never had children (although I have step-children.) But I have talked to many parents who confide that they've stopped.

Here's the thing about that: yes, it takes time, effort, and privacy. You might not be "in the mood." You may have other issues too, like not feeling desirable. And most of all, you're exhausted. I get that.

There are many times you're not in the mood or are too tired to do something, but that doesn't mean you get a pass. You can't just not go to work, or not do laundry, because you don't feel like it...at least not for long. Look at sex the same way.

There is a way to get sex back in your life.

First, "fake it till you make it." If you have gotten to the point where you don't really like having sex, that's okay, you can still do it.

Next, if it's just not feasible for the two of you to carve out alone time, then make a plan.

The reality check is that it is feasible, but you have to work harder, that's all. Start with a list of what needs to happen to make sex possible. If you're really exhausted, keep every single task separate, from "call mom about watching kids" to "talk to husband."

Brainstorm times to have sex. Think, afternoon naps. Or get a sitter. Call in sick. Make a date night and stick to it. If you can't stay up past 10:00, have a day date. Drop off the kids at your dad's and head home for some sexy time. But start it up.

Just like exercising for the first time in a while, you'll immediately experience the positive benefits of bringing sex back in your lives, and it'll get easier to do it.

What Do You Want?

What we want often turns up in our life, like a self-fulfilling prophecy. If we want to always be right, in our mind we will be, and that will cause problems. If we want a big house, often, we will get it. What we envision becomes reality. If we see ourselves as failing at relationships and life, we will.

It's important to step back and take a bird's eye view of what we want in life versus what we have.

Let me hazard a guess at what you would say that you want: You want to be happy. You want to have fun in your relationship. You want to be appreciated, respected, and understood. You want to truly feel good about who you are. Am I close?

Time to Think

Many of us do not take the time to think about these things. When we have spare brain time, we're usually doing something. We're looking at screens, listening to the radio, watching TV, taking the kids somewhere, playing games, making dinner, fixing something, sleeping, or thinking about a problem at work.

Rarely are we sitting around pondering: What is happening in my relationship? What do I want in life?

It isn't as though life encourages this quiet reflection. In fact, it's a challenge to carve out time just to think in the first place.

Proactive Preemptive Problem-Solving

If we do think about our life or our relationship, it's usually because problems have grown to the extent that they cannot be ignored. For instance, work is not going well. Or you are fighting a lot at home. Typically, most people have an "if it ain't broke, don't fix it" attitude towards everything: the gutter that is getting old, but still works; the child who is doing *well enough* in school, the wife who seems happy *enough*, etc.

When there's not a problem, we don't worry or pay close attention. It's when there is a severe issue that forces our attention that we begin thinking. There is a different way that will actually save you time and effort down the road, and that's taking time to be proactive and thoughtful about what you value.

Proactive thinkers spend time deciding what kind of life they want and then set about making it so, aligning their values with desired experiences. They work on things like their relationship daily, rather than waiting for times to get tough or stress to really take hold.

If we wait until problems emerge to look at ourselves and the way we behave, it's tougher to resolve. At this point, personality labels have been affixed, perceptions fixed, verbal arrows have hit their target, damage is everywhere. Sex is probably not happening (or not often), and meanwhile, we are still living our lives because we're all busy and life must go on.

Instinctively Being an Asshole

The times you act like an asshole often occur when you are reacting instinctively to something or someone around you. The way you act – snapping, shooting a harsh look, or ignoring someone, are behaviors and communication that you've perfected over your lifetime and for the most part they are automatic. So let's look closer at them.

Snapping at someone causes problems, regardless of whether they've snapped at you first. Snapping at someone means you've effectively ended respectful communication before it started.

It also damages relationships, especially over time, because who likes to be snapped at? Also if you snap on a regular basis, this adds to your partner's negative perception of you. The best thing you can do here is control your tongue. Think before you speak.

Taking a breath and thinking through what you want to say and the best way to say it will give you a better chance at being heard and understood correctly, not to mention a better chance at having a good conversation. It'll also help you avoid saying something you don't necessarily mean, like "How come you never listen to me?" Instead of an accusation it becomes conversational, "Oh, didn't you hear me?"

I want to acknowledge here that sometimes it feels as if we don't have control when we snap. I've been there. But that's just something you tell yourself. You really do have control over how you speak.

This is similar to people saying they can't help but interrupt people around them. Yes, you can. No one else is in control of your mouth. If you're honest, what you mean is that it is very hard for you to let someone else finish speaking before you chime in.

That is solvable, though. It just takes practice, patience, and determination to make this change. I've seen hundreds successfully stop interrupting through my training and teaching, including people diagnosed with ADHD.

A note on interruption: If you realize you interrupted someone, stop talking, apologize, and then let them finish talking. Because becoming aware when you interrupt is key, catching yourself, apologizing, and letting the other person finish reinforces your own awareness of your communication. It's also the right thing to do. If you forget what you were going to say (a common reason people interrupt) realize that you speaking and sharing what you think *right at that moment* is not actually the most important thing. The world won't stop revolving because you forgot what you were going to say. The most important person inside this conversation right at that moment is the *other* person – the one you are listening to. Having success in this arena is very freeing, but it will take work.

Snapping at someone operates using the same principle. Your thinking is your worst enemy, or best friend, depending on what you've decided about how much you can control yourself. So trust me, you can stop, think, and then talk, avoiding snapping altogether. If you do snap, apologize and start over.

Along these same lines, giving someone a harsh look or ignoring someone (because they are annoying you or you are too busy or overwhelmed by them or whatever the reason) has the same effect.

Over time exhibiting these behaviors earns you the label of asshole. Or an inconsiderate jerk. An unfeeling prick. Take your pick. The point is, someone who is ignored *feels* like you don't care. They think you're not invested, you don't understand them, and you don't care to understand them.

The above may or may not be true. But interestingly, Gottman's research reveals something different is often happening when one partner goes silent: you are so angry or frustrated that you are instinctively taking time to calm down. You are "flooded," which is a Gottman term that means you're in fight or flight mode.

And as I mentioned earlier, when you're angry or flooded, your creative thinking and nice communication go out the window. Your adrenaline shoots up. It actually is *not* possible to communicate nicely and effectively if you are flooded.

Make this Personal

Think of a recent time you've walked away from someone to avoid making it worse or because you were so overwhelmed or angry that you just did not know what to say. We often instinctively take the time we need to calm down because on some level we know that we can't communicate in this state.

Someone who acts out in that state rather than walking away – someone who doesn't notice what's happening and therefore doesn't bite their tongue – will instead be mean or belligerent because when we are flooded, we are reduced to the most elementary behaviors and communication.

And if you're flooded, and you walk away (essentially ignoring your partner), then she gets flooded, too, if she isn't already. Two flooded people trying to work it out are not good. Your hearing capacity is actually diminished too. If you do try to communicate while flooded, this is often when you say that thing you later regret, or do that thing you later regret.

Daniel Goleman talks about this a lot. It's the amygdala hijack I mentioned before, when the emotion center of our brains is taken over by intense, sudden feelings (often anger or fear.) Interestingly it actually takes longer for adrenaline to decrease in men than women. That's why it can be harder for men to calm down, Gottman has found. We are different physiologically.

So What Should You Do?

First, learn to recognize when you are feeling this way. You'll know because you feel flushed, angry, possibly misunderstood, you'll want to get away from who you are fighting with, and you can't think straight. Sometimes you'll repeat yourself in hopes that your partner will finally understand what you're saying after the eighth time you say it.

From now on, when you find yourself in this situation you need to put on the brakes. Take some time apart. When you're apart, don't think about the situation. Do something distracting and normal like reading a magazine or a book or watching television.

But – and this is key - what you definitely *should not* do is take a break without communicating it first. Tell your partner that you need some time apart – otherwise you make it worse because she'll think you are ignoring her. You're not. You're actually protecting the relationship by taking a break. More on this below.

When you are calmer (and she is, too) you'll be able to gain control of your emotions, think more clearly, and communicate in a way that doesn't damage the relationship.

Now you know how to recognize when you're flooded, and you know that when it happens, you should communicate and then take a break. If you want to maintain a better relationship, be happier, and not be an asshole in arguments, do this starting now. Your relationship will be better for it, and you'll both be happier.

The Break Signal

After recognizing when you feel flooded and that you should take a break to compose yourself, the next thing you need to know is how to communicate that you need a break.

Fortunately, it's not complicated. The way you communicate that you need a break depends on what feels natural to the two of you. Some people hold up a hand to signal "stop." Some people say "hey, let's take a break." It will depend on the two of you and what feels natural.

But it's important that you two talk about it and establish a shared signal *before* you are angry with each other. Your partner needs to understand what I described above, so he knows why it's important to *really* give you some time when you say you need a break. And the two of you need to agree to drop whatever is happening and take some space when one of you uses the break signal, no matter how upset you both are.

Some people (and you may be familiar with this behavior) will pursue communicating with you anyway. Hopefully by explaining why it is important not to do that, this won't happen with you. Forcing the two of you to communicate beyond the we-need-a-break point is destructive because at that point it's just pushing your buttons and will make the argument much worse, since you're both flooded. You'll get even more upset and more and more cloudy in your thinking, not to mention the stress levels in your body will continue to rise. And being repeatedly flooded over time is not only bad for you, it's bad for your relationship. You don't want to be anywhere near a person or situation in which you get repeatedly flooded.

From what I've seen in my work, this behavior, perpetuated over time, is one reason people break up. They try to get space or take a break, but they're never given it because the other person "needs" to talk. Regardless of how hard it feels to let it go, sometimes a break is necessary.

But...don't just drop or bury the disagreement. It's tempting to do so – after all, who really wants to revisit the horrible argument you just had? But you probably should revisit it. While you don't have to talk through every little thing, it's a good idea to talk through most things. I'll tell you how in a moment, but first, let's talk about why.

If I Ignore This, It'll Go Away

Not really. When we don't talk about challenging moments or arguments, it's not as though they go away or they are forgotten. We think about them even if we are unaware that we're doing so. Research shows that if we don't process these moments, then eventually in our minds we will come up with a label for the other person that explains their behavior.

So, over time if you repeatedly act rude, never apologize, and then don't talk about it, in your mind it may be forgotten. But in her mind, she's still making sense of it. And eventually she'll give you a negative label, like "asshole," simply because this helps her mind make sense of the way you act.

People who stuff their feelings inside and never talk about it when they are mad at their partner will know what this is like because eventually, you blow. When you blow, out comes whatever you've decided about them, whatever label you've affixed to them. "You're so selfish!" or "you're such a bitch!" etc. The recipient of this often has no idea where this is coming from, because you have not shared how you're feeling before.

When you do get into an uncomfortable spot and find yourself flooded, take that break; just remember, it's a good idea to talk again about whatever it is that you took a break from.

This is one of those things that may feel awkward at first, but like I said earlier, a lot of changes feel awkward at first. It won't be awkward once it is a habit. Later in the book, I'll dive deeper into how to talk about conflict.

Reality Check on Conflict

Did you know, around 70% of what you argue about over the lifetime of your relationship will *never* change? You'll still be arguing about the same things in 10 years. That's because you are two totally different people with a variety of attitudes, values, and beliefs, and those will not change.

For instance, if being on time is important to her that most likely will never change. If having a clean kitchen is important to you, this is unlikely to change.

Everyone knows one mistake we make is getting into a relationship thinking that the other person will change over time. For the most part, we don't change a lot. We do make incremental changes because we can't help but be influenced to an extent in relationship with another, and we also change as we mature. But as adults, who we are at the core – our attitudes and values and beliefs - won't change.

The 70% number above is also from Gottman's research with over 4,000 couples over forty-plus years. He terms these long-term arguments "perpetual" as they are always present. The other 30% he says are "solvable." You can fix them. These are often smaller things like whose family's house you will visit for a holiday or how you divvy up a chore.

Since 70% of what you argue about won't ever change, you need to stop trying to change each other and instead move into understanding, respecting, and living successfully with one another. To do this, you need to realize that just like you, your partner's ideas/beliefs/values are important.

This touches on the importance of respecting and learning from others, and something that if you habitually behave like an asshole, is hard for you to implement. One way you can show respect is fairly simple, and that is by listening in a deeper way.

Transformational Listening

Here is a try-at-home experiment.

Right now, pick something that you two consistently argue about in your head. Got it? Okay. Here's the listening experiment: the next time you talk about it your *only* goal is to more deeply understand her.

When she starts explaining her viewpoint and feelings, number one, just listen, and number two, ask good questions like "What does that look like for you?" or make thoughtful comments like: "That sounds awful. I think I understand, what you mean is... (rephrase what she said.)"

Although these may seem strange to do at first, they actually work to make her feel understood, provided you were listening and you correctly understood. If you didn't, ask more questions to clarify and try again.

Be a supportive listener, too. Say things like "That's interesting" or "I can imagine if I believed x to be true, I'd feel that way too."

Do not turn the tables and make it about you. Even if something she says raises your ire, resist giving your input. Keep your focus and the conversation on her.

I give this exercise to people I work with and most of them find out that when they put their own opinions and feelings to the side and focus 100% on the other person, they realize they never understood the other person in the first place. This is because they never really listened. They were too focused on their own thoughts and feelings or on being right.

Often when you do this, when you fully listen and attempt to really understand, especially about something you do not agree on, your other half will eventually (sometimes right away) begin to mirror your behavior and end up listening to you more fully, and wanting to understand you, too.

I refer to this as transformational listening. Your listening and communicative experience literally transforms into something much more meaningful, deep, and connected.

Practice "Transformational" Listening

When this kind of listening happens and we allow for it, then empathy blooms. The good news is, it's really hard to be assholes to each other when you feel empathetic. And empathy happens *inside of* feeling understood.

When we have empathy for another, it's easier for us to overlook whatever we are arguing about; it's easier to cut the other person some slack; and it's easier to let the other person be her natural self without being bothered by as much by it or taking it personally.

I want to emphasize that when you try this at home, remember, you do not need to agree with her. I run into this over and over again. One reason we feel like we can't fully listen to another person is that THEY ARE WRONG. It is SO obvious.

That may be true. It doesn't matter. Who is wrong and who is right is not the point. It's okay to let them be "wrong" and by listening, you don't need to change your mind. It's not about you. It's about them, and understanding them.

Let it sink in that you don't need to change your opinion at all. Just because you listen and you try to understand does not mean you will agree. It simply means you are committed to trying to understand another. The supportive statement, "I can imagine if I believed x to be true, I'd feel that way, too" is a great thing to say when you don't agree. You can still envision how, if you were like the person you are listening to and had the same thoughts and feelings, you'd feel that way, too. It's stepping into another's shoes, as completely as possible.

I cannot possibly know what you have to learn during your life from your partner, but you do have things to learn that are unique to you and your relationship, just like he or she has things to learn from you. But to really grow, we need to learn to put ourselves on the back burner at times, and just be present with someone and listen. Then we'll be able to understand our partner more and we'll be able to respectfully talk about something we couldn't have before. Not to mention, when we just listen, sharing about day-to-day stress happens more easily.

When you do the above exercise effectively, your communication will improve. You and your lover will feel, and be, closer. When you experience these new positive interactions, you'll want to apply this kind of listening to every conversation you have. Just remember it does take work, effort, and patience with yourself. Keep at it until it's the new normal. The rewards you two will eventually experience are hard to fully describe in words.

Put Yourself in Their Shoes

Let's back up for a minute here. In reality, you can't truly understand anyone until you first, fully listen to them, and second, try to understand what they're saying *from their perspective*. This is the second and most important part of listening in a transformational way.

Listening in this transformational state is a skill. As I said, it takes time, repeated effort, patience, and practice. You may be tempted to think it's too hard, but it isn't. Just press on and don't give up. Trust me, I used to be a full-time interrupter and I was extremely caught up in and distracted by my own thoughts. I've known many, many people who had those same patterns. I overcame this and other negative listening behaviors, and so did they. You can do it.

Think of increasing empathy as your goal right now. Your friendship is the strong bond that holds your relationship together, which is why I repeatedly refer to your partner as your friend. If you think about it, having and showing empathy is just being a friend to your partner. It's really that simple.

But you have to be able to tamp down your own self-interest in the moment and your instinctual communication habits, like interrupting or judging her in your mind (therefore not listening fully.)

Don't get distracted by your own thoughts demanding attention. The way to do this is to NOT beat yourself up for having thoughts come through. Notice them, but then focus your attention on your partner. Focus and re-focus and re-focus until your attention is 100%

fixed on the other person.

The more you do this, the more your thoughts won't make such a ruckus in your brain. It'll get easier to use all of your attention and be present in a conversation. Moreover, once you've gotten to the point of being able to dismiss thoughts and bring your focus back to your partner, you will experience the great benefits of listening like this and you will change. It will no longer be hard. All the work I described becomes effortless, your new normal. It'll be a habit.

Trust also that your lover will return the favor. If not right away, eventually. You'll be acting different and communicating more respectfully, and most people respond to this. Of course, there are exceptions. For instance, if your partner has also become a total asshole and is unaware of it, she may never change because she's stuck. If her perception of you and how you are is really entrenched, don't expect immediate results.

But don't throw in the towel. Keep up the good listening and communicative behavior.

So You're with an Asshole

Let me make something clear before I get into this part. First, if you are being physically, mentally, or emotionally abused you already know it's best to get OUT of that situation.

I've been there. Not the physical abuse, but mental and emotional abuse. I was stuck in that. And that's what it's like - being stuck. Well-intentioned people around me would tell me what to do or what they would do in my situation whenever they got a chance. But they may as well have been talking to a wall because I wasn't ready to act on any of those truths.

Of course in the end they were right. It's just that I had to get there myself.

One type of support that *really* helped me during that relationship was having someone in my life who simply believed in ME, was patient with me, and listened to me. She would tell me, "Sarah, I know you'll figure this out. You'll get through this. I have faith in you." She told me that repeatedly. And eventually when I'd had enough, I drew courage from her words and I did get out.

To this day I am so thankful for that relationship because being in it taught me many things, including that *anyone* can get stuck in a bad relationship. I was (and am) a strong woman. Not only that, because of my training and work, I'm more knowledgeable than most about relationships (including codependent ones like that one was) and communication. And I got stuck! Anyone can get stuck.

Since the days when my friends told me those truths and impatiently watched me get treated badly, some of them later became involved in bad relationships. They're out of them now, but the point is lots of people go through this, and not many people talk about it. It can happen to anyone.

The other reason I'm grateful for that relationship is because for whatever reason, being torn down over time like that made me come out on the other end with an unshakeable foundation. I am so much stronger now and know my worth. I was done feeling bad and questioning myself. I developed this inner strength that radiated out of me. And when I met the man who later became my husband, I was ready.

The funny thing about this time is that looking back on myself in that relationship, the truth was I did not believe that I was worth more than how he treated me. Of course, at the time, I would've sworn to you that I thought highly of myself. But in reality I didn't because my actions (staying in the relationship) did not line up with that truth. It was only when I really learned what it felt like to be emotionally strong and have healthy self-esteem that I realized I never actually believed in my own worth before.

And the other huge thing is that I didn't come to actually believe these positive things about myself until AFTER I left the relationship. I took a physical, raw, scary leap of faith into the "unknown," letting go of what was comfortable and familiar at the time...a relationship that was horrible, but at least I knew what to expect. It was scary facing that unknown future and trusting that I'd be better for it. After all, I was used to the roller coaster our relationship was - full of ups and downs, but predictable. But after I took action, only then did I finally believe all the good positive things about myself that I lost sight of inside of that relationship.

The point to this is, we don't have to have our feelings back us up to take a correcting course of action. Just do what you need to do when you are able to. Your feelings will follow and after you take action, you'll "feel" like you did the right thing, and as though you are truly worth more. This isn't just my experience, it is the experience of many people I've talked with.

Of course when you do this, know it won't become all rainbows and sunshine because you made a move forward. It can be hard, but so is much of life and growth.

This section of the book is for those of you who love someone and have no plans to leave, but want to make it better as far as you are able. I can help with that. But first I wanted to tell you a little of my story, and emphasize that yes, I coach people, but I am NOT a counselor (and I'd highly recommend seeing one or working with a coach who is right for you. It's helpful.)

Only you know what kind of situation you are in and whether you should stay or go. Like me, you will figure it out. *I believe in you.*

So let's get started. First of all, when you've decided the person you're with is an asshole in general, rather than in specific or limited situations, then you have some work to do. Both of you do.

You cannot actually set out to change another person (that's controlling!), but you can change yourself and how you think through learning new communication skills. And some change is inevitable, because you do have influence on your partner.

Take It Back to the Beginning

Think back to when you two were friends. Or to the beginning of your relationship when the honeymoon phase was in full swing. When your relationship has deteriorated, when you say your partner is an asshole, your friendship is at risk, and so is your future together.

Love may get all the glory, but friendship is ultimately what keeps us together – or together and happy, I should say. Some couples stay together and live separate lives without any semblance of a friendship. All of Gottman's research led to a key finding: it's the quality of a couple's friendship that makes or breaks their future together.

It's also about learning to fight nicely and be proactive in maintaining what you do have.

First, you need to do anything that will strengthen your friendship. Because our interactions train our brains to only "see" our partner's actions as mostly positive or negative (depending on how our relationship is going), it's not as simple as "talking" ourselves into seeing what we can't see.

Rather than simply trying to will yourself to quash your negative perception of your partner, flip that and take action instead. Proactively build upon the positive things you *do* have and you *can* see. Start again and re-build your friendship.

What does building your friendship actually entail? Think about how you'd approach someone you just met that you really want to be friends with. You ask them about their day and their life, you confide in each other, support one another, and have fun together. You don't judge them. You laugh with them. You respond to messages. You cut them slack when they're not the perfect friend; you don't keep track of how they could've been a better friend. You care.

Do those things with your partner. Do them *until you notice a change*, and do them without keeping score.

Deepen Your Friendship

Going beyond the above, think proactively about what you'd like to know and discover about your partner.

When I was younger I ran a youth camping trip, and I created an icebreaker game for us to get to know each other. Everyone wrote down a question and put the questions in a basket; then we passed them around and took turns answering them. They ranged from "what was the worst haircut you've ever had" to "what would you spend your life doing if you didn't have to make money for any reason" (the latter is my favorite question to ask people, so yes, that one was mine.) We laughed a lot and got to know each other pretty quickly playing this question game.

Think of some fun questions and then on your next date, or uninterrupted conversation, ask your partner one or two (or a few.) After we've been with someone for a long time, we know them pretty well.

We tend to stop discovering who they are and what they think. Instead, we get stuck in those "how was your day?" and "what's on the schedule for this weekend" conversations. These, of course are fine, but rich relationships are a combination of mundane and not-so-mundane conversations. To shift from mundane to not-so-mundane, you'll want to be more intentional with your questions, and go deeper to reignite the friendship and intimacy in your relationship.

Think of these questions as conversation starters and ways to get to know each other better; this is also a way to cultivate an attitude of curiosity regarding our partner and check our assumptions as well. How well do you really know each other?

The more open-ended the questions, the better. For instance, a closed question is "what's your favorite color to wear?" and an open-ended question is "If you wanted to do one thing in your life over again and do it differently, what would it be and why?" Open-ended questions often use "how" or "why." They are well thought-out questions that take time to think about and answer. The whole idea is to get the other person to talk and reveal more of themselves.

Truthfully, we don't know each other 100% completely. There are all kinds of thoughts that are often not shared, so approach your partner like you did when you were first dating and you wanted to know everything about him. Those conversations bonded you then, and they will again.

Gottman also has a similar exercise called "Love Maps" in which questions are created for you. This is a *really* fun exercise. You can buy the physical cards or the phone app (at the time of this writing, it's only available for iPhones) and do this on a date.

I told a guy who works at a local deli near where I live about the Love Maps exercise. He and his girlfriend did the exercise that night, and when I saw him next he was all smiles. Rather than go to the party they were supposed to attend that night, they stayed up until 3 AM doing the Love Maps exercise and drinking wine. It's that fun.

Being Proactive

The more you proactively build your friendship, the better. Building your friendship also means your respect for one another will grow, and asshole treatment will decrease.

Just as meditating does a bunch of positive things for your brain and well-being, doing positive things like spending quality time together, asking deeper questions, and having fun together does a world of good for your relationship.

I'll talk more extensively about trust and respect in the workplace part of the book, but it's worth mentioning here, too. Each of us wants to be respected. And trusted. These are crucial pillars in a healthy relationship.

But when one isn't there, notice how the other tends to take a nosedive, too. Say for instance you act in an untrustworthy manner and your husband finds out about it. There goes his trust for you. Not only now do you have an act of betrayal to deal with, but his respect for you has decreased, as well.

It can be a really long road to get back trust, but it's a road that both of you must travel. It's not just about the person who betrayed you – the person who tries to fix it by groveling, apologizing, and generally feeling like crap with only a small shred of hope that she can be forgiven. It's also about being able to talk about it when necessary, and him being willing to forgive you – as best as he can. He may need to repeatedly forgive you as the betrayal continues to sting. This takes time and patience on both ends.

And for God's sake, do not do whatever caused this betrayal in the first place again.

On a related note, it's imperative to realize we all have certain weaknesses. They could be a weakness for another person, a terrible habit, or our judgmental nature. Know your weakness – the big one that threatens your relationship - and don't feed it. For example, if you have an ex who repeatedly resurfaces in your life, realize that this person is going to keep popping up until YOU get the point of this "lesson" in your life and you turn away.

You have to decide, though. Life has a way of continually offering the same lessons of growth and choice until you finally learn.

Let's get back to being proactive and talk about fighting.

Similar to when I mentioned snapping, when you have a complaint about your partner or something he did or didn't do, regardless of whether it's valid or not, give some thought to *how* you approach him before you approach him. This requires you to stop and think first, again being proactive.

First, think about the current circumstances and his state of mind. Is this a time when he's generally tired? Stressed? Overwhelmed? Put yourself in his shoes and figure out the ideal time to talk. Maybe it's not in the morning as you're both headed to work, for instance. You'll have better success if you get the timing right.

Then, and this is the most important, watch what you say *and* how you say it. Keep it specific rather than general. Saying you "always" or you "never" do this or that is like throwing a huge communication porcupine at someone when you really wanted them to catch a soft cuddly animal. The former will make your partner feel attacked. Instead, communicate only about that specific thing.

Here's an example of specific communication: "I noticed you didn't talk to my sister last night at our family dinner. I told you she's been feeling left out and was hoping you'd help her feel part of things by talking with her."

Communication Porcupine: "Why don't you *ever* listen to me? I told you my sister is having issues feeling left out, and you didn't even bother to talk to her last night. You have *never* cared for her like I want you to."

You can see why the former would create an actual conversation, while the latter would send your partner into a defensive tailspin.

After you've given your communication habits some thought, the next step is to have meaningful, responsibility-taking conversations.

Recognize Defensiveness

Even if use precise phrasing during your communication, in order to have a more successful conversation, you still need to watch for and handle defensiveness from your other half. To do this you must recognize defensiveness for what it is conveying. Let me explain.

One of the ways someone demonstrates defensiveness is by playing the innocent victim. In response to your thoughtfully worded and timed issue, he responds with "You always criticize me! I can never do anything right!" And suddenly rather than discussing the topic you introduced, the focus has shifted to him. You are concerned about his feelings and you respond to that, instead.

But what happens to the original issue? It's lost. This kind of a response is a form of defensiveness. Don't fall for it. Recognize it and deal with it then and there. I'll tell you how in a minute.

When I'm working with people on this I tell them not to be mad at their partner for pulling the innocent victim card. It's usually not premeditated. Often they don't realize what they're doing, and that this response generally makes things worse.

This is a communication behavior we often learned in childhood. It's a way to avoid taking responsibility, and back then it worked. Think back to when your parent asked you to do something, and you didn't want to. One example of this is when we pretended something hurt and said we couldn't vacuum (or whatever was being asked of us) because "suddenly" we weren't feeling well. Our parents then became more concerned about our overall well-being and forgot about what they'd originally asked of us. The bottom line is, this behavior is manipulative. Many of us learned it then, and took it with us.

So, how should you handle this? When you recognize that it's happening, don't get caught up in it. Don't take the bait. Keep the conversation on topic. You can respond by acknowledging what he said and redirecting. "That's not my intention and we can talk about that, but let's finish talking about this other thing first." The key is to re-focus immediately on what you brought up and not get deterred.

A real slippery communicator (or someone being an asshole) will continue to try to shift your focus away from what you just said and then before you know it, you're in a fight. Just recognize this if it continues to happen. If it does, I'd recommend cooling off for a while and when you're both calm, talk to your partner about how you want to argue going forward. Let him know that you need to be able to finish a conversation and stay on a topic.

Suggest that the two of you can "parking lot" other issues that come up so he doesn't feel as though you don't care about these other things he's mentioned. It's your choice as to whether you want to bring up his unconscious way of diverting responsibility.

"Parking lot" is a term used in a meeting environment, when participants bring up topics outside the meeting's focus. When you "parking lot" an off-agenda topic, you write down the topics or comment to address later, then continue with your agenda topics.

Finally, there's your tone. Do NOT start off snappy or mean. I'm sure you've heard that it's not what you say, but how you say it. So really, really, be kind and don't approach this conversation until you really can be kind. It's almost impossible to have a productive conversation after you've started off poorly.

All of this takes restraint, planning, and practice. But if you think it through ahead of time then you can put it into practice with ease when the situation arises.

So You've Been Silenced

When an asshole doesn't want you to discuss something of a difficult nature with him, often he says mean things that have the effect of shutting you down and shaming you. For instance, you may be upset about something and bring it up, only to have him yell at you for being upset. What happens then? You feel even more upset – and before you know it, you're flooded. You feel not heard, misunderstood, disrespected, and possibly, ashamed.

If this happens, take some time apart to calm down separately as I mentioned previously. After you're calm, then recognize what you are feeling and talk yourself through it, or validate yourself. I'll validate you too: it is *completely normal* to get upset and freak out sometimes. We all do this.

Even if, in retrospect, you agree that you shouldn't have gotten so upset, remember, we all overreact from time to time. After all, each of us have buttons that get pushed and things that bother us particularly, but go unnoticed by others. None of us are perfect.

The effect of being silenced by a lover can go even further if the person being silenced then also feels shame on top of it. Think back to being a child: many of us as children were chastised for being upset about something. The result was the same as it is today – we felt that our anger was not okay.

So recognize when you feel ashamed and validate yourself, even if he won't validate you. It's important to be honest with yourself and recognize that whatever you are feeling is perfectly acceptable. Simply get clear about how you are feeling, and just sit with it. Don't try to talk yourself out of it or change it. And don't slip into judging yourself.

What about the asshole in this communication pattern? How does he change? First, the asshole needs to recognize the effect of yelling at you: you feel silenced and shamed. By yelling at you, essentially he is communicating to you that what you feel and who you are is not okay.

Next, the asshole needs time apart from you as well. Once he is calm he will be able to go further and practice making communicative changes the next time this happens.

When a person is flooded (and perhaps acting like an asshole because of this) it's very hard to recognize and break down what is happening in that moment, but when you both take time to calm down, it will be easier to see what happened in retrospect.

After calming down, you both will be able to look back on the chain of events and how what just happened led to shaming and silencing. This anger-shame dance is a communication pattern that many people enact unconsciously. You'll recognize it happening when you notice the warning signs: you've just been yelled at and you feel bad about yourself and your relationship.

Once you both calm down and are able to talk through the exchange again, then it's the asshole's turn to apologize and take responsibility for being mean. When the apology has been offered, your response is to accept it. Then move on.

Also remember, practice makes perfect. As you recognize and change communicative patterns realize that you are both trying the best you can. Have patience with yourselves and each other throughout this process. Be quick to forgive.

When one person is upset and brings something up to another person, it's the responsibility of the person hearing the complaint to look past their own feelings and focus on the concern they should have for the other person. Said another way: focus on the empathy you feel for your partner and *not your own reaction* to what was said. Typically people don't get upset over nothing, so it's best to resolve the issue.

Try to understand what is happening and address it calmly, rather than reacting explosively to the person who shared their feelings.

Even if you don't agree with the person who is upset, that's okay. You are not them, and just because you wouldn't get upset about a particular action or comment doesn't mean they wouldn't. We get upset over different things.

Learning to practice this empathy (while forgetting your own interests for the moment) will go a long way towards helping you talk through difficult issues and in the end, each of you will be able to understand the other a little more.

Most importantly, your partner will feel heard, understood, respected, and accepted. She may not need you to agree or even understand completely, as long as she experiences these things.

Corrosive Acid in a Relationship

I truly believe that it's possible to stay in a relationship with someone who has asshole tendencies IF they recognize this and they also care about and respect you.

The relationship is doomed however, when an asshole is dripping in contempt toward you *all of the time*. That's because he no longer respects you. When your partner does not view you as an equal and feels contempt constantly, it just doesn't work. There are things you can do to try to change this, though.

But first, imagine for a moment, your best friend. What if your best friend didn't respect you and looked down on you? That friendship wouldn't make it, right? You'd have no trouble getting rid of a friend who treats you like you are "less than." With relationships, however, it's trickier.

Gottman found that pervasive contempt toward one

another in relationships is the number one predictor of divorce. (Occasionally feeling contempt towards your partner isn't a relationship death sentence, but continual contempt probably is.) Contempt comes from negative thoughts that have been percolating in your mind for a long time. Or from negative beliefs you've formed and held onto.

If you want a different result in your relationship, first focus on proactively communicating and re-building your friendship. Next, become aware of how you are thinking about your relationship and work to dwell mostly on the positive thoughts. Through your behavior (actions) and awareness of your thoughts, your positive feelings will follow.

It's interesting to me that often when I first start working with people, they believe they "can't help" what goes through their mind and how they handle their thoughts. You can. It just takes awareness, practice, and time. And more importantly, no matter what goes through your mind, you can practice not entertaining the thought, if it's counterproductive. Mindfulness practices are a HUGE help when it comes to this.

Here's an example of noticing your negative thoughts about your partner and taking control. Let's say, for instance, that you think he's thoughtless. He's an asshole. What is something you believe about your partner that's negative?

Take your thought or belief, and put it into the "light of day" and ask yourself honestly, does *every experience* I have with him line up with this characterization? Is it really always true? Maybe it's true sometimes, but my guess is that it's not true all of the time.

It's also helpful to say out loud what you believe. Hearing yourself say something aloud will be more powerful than if you just think it.

If you take my example, he's thoughtless, then from now on, notice when he IS thoughtful and actually say something to recognize that. It could be the smallest thing, like asking about your day. Much like training a child by recognizing positive behaviors, start looking for and commenting on the things he does that you appreciate. What we focus on grows, whether it's a positive or a negative behavior. Plus, when we focus on negative things, we tend to notice them and only them. It's a bad deal all around. And the unfortunate outcome is that he may do many thoughtful things, but if you have a negative mindset towards him, you won't see half of them, like I said earlier in the book. So start being intentional about finding the positive.

In addition to acknowledging positive things, take it a step further, and try dwelling on them in your mind. ("It was so nice this morning when he scraped the snow off my car. That was so thoughtful.") Say it out loud. Say it again. Feel the happiness and thankful feeling that comes as you dwell on it.

Just a side note: I'm not suggesting that you ignore the reality of his behavior if he's very mean or abusive. Like I said earlier, you are the one who knows how far things have gone and whether you need to just get out. But if you are feeling "stuck" in your negative thinking and patterns with him, start by changing your thoughts about him, then change your behavior by noticing and commenting on the good things when they happen. This will go a long way toward recreating your strong friendship.

You can also take this further by doing things for him. If you're familiar with the five love languages theory by author Gary Chapman you know that a lot of men value "acts of service" and "physical touch." This is a way they often show they love you, by doing things for you. It's also what many of them like – to have things done for them. Look for ways you can lighten his load and do things for him, or give him a back rub.

Do NOT keep track of whether or how often he reciprocates. When we keep track, we are inadvertently biased so there's really no point to it, except to rekindle your anger toward your partner. Just add positive bricks to continue building the foundation of your relationship. You do this by using the communication tips in this book, and by recognizing and dwelling on positive behaviors and your friendship. There ARE things you can do to make your relationship better, and beyond that, keep in mind that you're also not perfect.

If you cringed when I mentioned contempt and a lack of respect because you recognize that this is how you're being treated, then I highly recommend the book by Patricia Evans, "The Verbally Abusive Relationship: How to Recognize it and How to Respond." This book unpacks the different ways someone who is verbally abusive uses communication to manipulate his or her partner. I'll give you a hint...for them, it's not about communicating.

Part 3 - Assholes in the Workplace

Let's start with assholes in power. Assholes in power are often in place for some combination of these three reasons: They're really good at the actual job they do and they got promoted because of this; they are friends with the right people who influenced or determined their position; or they've managed to put on a good front so the people who have power over them don't realize that they have a terrible personality.

Often people who've put the asshole in the position of power do not realize just how detrimental it is to leave him there. (Again, the asshole could be a woman, but for consistency, I'm using the male pronoun.)

Because this is not a long book, I am simply offering my observations. They are informed by my education, teaching, and work experience both within my communication training and coaching practice, and in other areas I've worked, including sales, marketing, accounting, and work with nonprofits.

What does an asshole look like in a workplace? What can you do about them, and what should you consider if you're working for one? What if you hired or promoted one? And finally, what if *you* are being the asshole?

What an Asshole Looks Like in the Workplace

An asshole, at their core, demonstrates disrespect towards others. At work, the assholes also have the power that comes with their position. When a power difference is added to any relationship, it becomes inherently more complicated.

And just because an asshole isn't technically in a position of authority doesn't mean he can't still use power. Every one of us has power; some of us just choose to use it differently. We can use it indirectly by choosing to remain silent; we can be uncooperative or disagreeable. Or, we can directly impact a situation by sharing our thoughts vocally.

Here's a scenario of someone who doesn't have positional authority, but uses his power nonetheless: Imagine being in a meeting with someone who talks over you constantly, shoots you insulting looks when you share an idea, and gossips about you behind your back. That's an asshole using his personal power to be a jerk to you (also known as bullying).

This person who is being an asshole may embody any of the following characteristics and more:

- Someone who doesn't care about or remember his employees' personal issues/lives.
- Someone who micro-manages, who displays lack of trust in those who work for him.
- Someone who talks negatively about people in your workplace.
- Someone who is closed-minded - often an asshole isn't open to hearing things that are contrary to his thoughts or ways of doing things. The asshole thinks a lot of himself.

We've all dealt with someone like this, whether it's in our own family around the dinner table or the annoying jerk in the corner office.

The *total* asshole (high on the asshole behavior continuum) may also frequently express impatience and doesn't think about how he communicates with others. For instance, he may believe that he communicates effectively but really he hasn't given this much thought, and doesn't care how he's perceived, therefore he is short with, or tends to snap at, some people.

When employees feel that they are working for someone who they view as an asshole, not only are they not as productive as they could be, but they aren't likely to stay, either. If they do stay but they are actively disengaged, morale and the company suffers. People learn to walk on eggshells around assholes.

Asshole Effect on the Company

When employees work for someone who acts like an asshole, this results in higher turnover, lower motivation, more sick days, unhappy workers, and ultimately, a negative impact on the company's bottom line.

It pays – in higher profits - for companies to have employees who are engaged, who *want to* stay, and who don't have to answer to an asshole.

Most employees start out committed and with a positive attitude about their company. And if you have employees who truly enjoy their job and feel empowered to do it well, they will thrive and in turn, they'll give their best to what they do. This also means you'll have and keep more customers.

So how do we end up with assholes in leadership?
Many people get promoted for the wrong reasons.
They may have excelled in their previous role, but
like I said before if it didn't involve managing people
they have no prior experience with this - so after
they've been promoted, they run into trouble.
Because they received a promotion as a reward, they
are now faced with having to figure out how to
manage people effectively. Leading people is an
important managerial skillset in itself. Anyone who
has ever led a team can attest to this.

In this new leadership role they may keep profits up,
but over time turnover rises. Watercooler gossip tells
the real story of how employees feel about their
leader.

Many things factor into a company's success or
failure, but employees and their impact matter a lot.
If your company has terrible customer service for
instance, your employees are not building
relationships with the customers. Unless you have a
monopoly in a particular service or product, there's
no reason customers will continue to bring you their
business.

I cannot tell you how many stories I've heard from
employees on the front lines who have valuable
advice to help the company do better, but they've
never been asked. In fact, they are silenced subtly or
overtly. Those that stay toe the line and learn to
keep their mouths shut, all the while fuming inside.
I've heard similar complaints from managers about
the people above them.

Employees care more about their work and work *much* harder if they feel valued and respected. For instance, you may hire someone with a great work ethic who goes above and beyond his job duties - but if that person is managed by someone who doesn't understand how to respect and develop employees, then that same employee will feel deflated, and over time will care less and less. To survive in a fast-changing business world, employees, their work and ideas are all vital assets to nurture.

When an asshole is running the ship or any part of the ship, employee loyalty decreases over time, turnover increases, and employees slowly lose respect for their boss and ultimately the company as a whole. After all, we tend not to respect someone who doesn't respect us.

Human Resources Meets Reality

Unfortunately employees often won't say anything to Human Resources, to you if you're in a management role, or to other people in positions of authority, because they believe to do so would be suicide for their career at that company. Not to mention, many people are conflict-averse, especially at work. This is just the way it is.

Personally, I find this unfortunate for many reasons. A good Human Resources department will help an employee *and* truly keep confidences – they are actually required to (except in certain scenarios). It is often the *perception of consequences*, not the consequences themselves, which keep employees from talking to HR.

So You Hired an Asshole - What Can You Do?

First, create the culture you say you have on your company website. If you have an open-door policy, then make that clear with your actions. Practice "management by walking around." There's no reason to wait for an employee to bring an issue to your door. Periodically invite them in for one-on-one conversations. And keep what they tell you confidential. If you say you're available to talk, actually carve out time to listen.

Second, cultivate the trust of your front-line employees. Ask them about their life, remember what they say, and follow up with them later. Just because you have a middle manager or director who isn't great with people doesn't mean you can't improve the climate at your company yourself. Also, ask them regularly and directly for their ideas on how to improve the workplace, how to streamline processes, and what is and isn't working. This makes them feel valued. And then consider what they say.

Third, pay close attention to how the person you suspect is an asshole communicates with and treats others. Observe others' reactions to him. This will give you hints as to how he is perceived. This may be challenging as you are likely to be the person he treats very well, so you need to see beyond that. One way to do this, aside from slinking around corridors and spying, is to set up an anonymous employee complaint system. But even that has limited value. People often don't trust these mechanisms to be anonymous, or fear that what they say may "out" them as the whistleblower.

Your best bet is to pay close attention to what's "really" happening around you in the company, and work to build your own relationships. Eventually, you will learn important truths.

Changing Accountability

Hold your managers accountable for the level of employee engagement in your organization. Make sure they are doing things like spending quality time with their employees and are working actively to build and maintain positive relationships. This could be anything from team-building exercises to taking one employee out for lunch every Friday. Ensure they are really able to take time to do this too.

Make sure managers tell you not only what's going well in their area, but also what needs to improve. But, and this is so important, to make this a reality, you need to ensure that your manager feels *safe* confiding in you. So, pay attention to how you respond when managers tell you what's not going well and resist the urge to respond punitively. The staff isn't showing up to work on time? Dock their pay! No. Try to understand the whole situation. Step back and analyze the big picture. Things like this always happen in a larger context. Also, people typically don't respond well to punitive communication or behaviors directed at them.

Your primary role at first in this scenario is to listen, not fix. Find out what's not going well, but also look for the factors contributing to the situation. If people aren't communicating in a timely fashion, why might that be? Is it because some people are not checking their email? Why aren't they checking it? Are they overworked, having to be away from the computer much of the time so that it's difficult for them to communicate via email? There are a lot of factors that can only be discovered when you have a full understanding of all the dynamics and people involved, and when you make it safe enough to discuss what the real problems are.

So first, listen. Ask probing questions to discover the reason(s) behind behaviors as well as to learn more about the manager's perception and solutions – for instance, it's very possible she brainstormed and maybe tried some solutions, as well as thought of next steps. Don't assume she has or hasn't, but be sure to find out as you approach her with an attitude of curiosity and exploration (not critical and closed-minded). This inquiry of the manager will also make her feel heard, understood, valued, and will reinforce that you two are on the same team. And you are. You are both human beings, just in different positions, but both trying to do what's best for employees and the company as a whole. Besides, people (managers, but anyone) like to feel like you value them and trust them to manage employees, even if they have made some mistakes.

Following your example, make sure managers are asking their employees how to improve the workplace, and really listening when employees share. Employees at every level want to feel that they are trusted and valued. So - not only should you model this behavior, but you should also explain what you are doing (watch your tone – don't be condescending), how you are communicating intentionally, and how she in turn could try approaching her employees.

When you have the right people doing the right jobs,

your company flourishes. Engaged employees stay longer, work harder and will feel passionate about your organization, which helps them be more creative and in turn affects innovation at work. But if they are stifled, micromanaged, treated poorly, and mistrusted, your organization suffers. There are also more instances of suits being brought against organizations when an employee isn't happy.

Gallup's 2013 American Workplace Report (covering 100 million workers) is worth reading for further information on how poor leadership affects employees. Their research found that 70% of U.S. employees are not engaged in their work <u>due to poor leadership</u>.

Think about it – that's 7 out of 10 employees. 50% of these disengaged workers just don't care. They are emotionally disconnected. The other 20% are what Gallup terms "actively disengaged." They are poison to an organization because they actively work to undermine it. They are the ones who disrupt meetings, spark conflict, and gossip negatively about their workplace to anyone who will listen. They are the ones other people complain about. For obvious reasons, disengaged employees are detrimental to an organization. But here are the numbers: Gallup estimates they cause between $450 and $550 billion – yes BILLION – in lost profits a year.

In my view, the most dangerous employees are the emotionally disconnected 50%. Typically we are aware of the 20%, and can take steps to either help them be more engaged and better employees, move them on to a better fit at another company, or get them a personal coach (if they are open to growth, hiring someone to coach them is a good idea because you already invested in them and they may become an amazing employee with the right kind of help.) But the disconnected 50% are more dangerous because you may not realize they aren't engaged. They do enough to avoid corrective action, but they don't stand out and they definitely don't shine. Because you don't notice them, they are like a slow-growing cancer in your organization. Alternately, you could have employees who really thrive in their work and relish the workplace. Those employees are what make your entire organization flourish.

Gallup and other researchers have found that employees don't leave companies, they leave managers. While there are many deficiencies among managers, one type of bad manager is the asshole.

What if You Work for an Asshole?

What to do if you're working for an asshole? That depends on your goals. Do you want to stay working in this field? At this company? If so, you must be extremely careful in how you handle this situation.

It's never a good idea to gossip or vent about this person, but often, you will feel the need to talk about what's happening. If you do feel this need, keep your complaints to a trustworthy non-coworker. This is a perfect time to rely on your support system.

According to Gottman's research, it is beneficial to have someone who will listen to you talk through your stresses. But the urge to talk about your misery should be tempered. According to other research (see the books *The Dance of Anger* and *Anger, the Misunderstood Emotion*), when we go on and on about something or someone, or ruminate over something we are angry about, we actually get angrier. There's no cathartic release for anger.

This research may seem like it's conflicting at first glance, but it isn't. That's because there's a difference between ruminating about an angering situation and sharing something that you're angry about, in order to explore and evaluate solutions. The latter is healthy and good.

Do's & Don'ts

At work, make sure you do show respect to your asshole boss, regardless of how you are treated. You can fake it if necessary. Note that showing respect does NOT mean you should accept unreasonable behavior or abuse. In fact, he will respect you even less if he believes that you are submissive when brazenly mistreated.

Do your job, do it well, keep records of what you do well, and keep your personal distance. This last bit of advice won't be difficult because the person you work for typically isn't interested in you, only himself.

While keeping personal distance, stick to personal and professional boundaries. Evaluate what you are comfortable sharing, and don't share more than that. When it comes to professional information as well, don't share too much; share only what others need to know to do their jobs effectively. If you are being micro-managed, rather than telling your supervisor about every little thing you do (feeding their need to micro-manage) instead share the results of what you are doing. It's harder to micro-manage someone who gets the job done, but doesn't report all the details.

Realize too, that sometimes you inadvertently helped to create the problem. Perhaps when you first started working at your job, you really wanted to exceed expectations, so you responded to your boss immediately. But now that time has passed, you feel that you've proven your worth and now you'd prefer to respond to your boss's requests in a more measured timeframe...which means not answering emails at 10pm.

I compare this problem to young adults in a brand new relationship. At first, the two of them text constantly throughout the day, responding to each other within seconds (ah, the honeymoon phase.) Eventually if the relationship continues, one half of the couple often no longer feels the need to respond to text messages within seconds. However, that person has just spent a year training their significant other that they respond instantaneously. Creating new expectations can be a painful process - I've even seen young adults break up over this issue.

We can face similar challenges in the workplace. After a work "honeymoon phase," we, too, want to make our work more manageable and not respond to every request immediately. For most jobs, immediate responses are not actually necessary. The good news is that with issues like emailing or working all hours, you can slowly re-train your supervisor.

For those in a supervisory role, you may not realize that by sending emails to team members late at night, you are creating an expectation that you require a response outside work hours. "I expect you will answer this" and "If I'm working, you should be too" is what employees often think you are communicating.

If you want to avoid putting unnecessary pressure on your staff, you could use an email tool to send your nighttime messages out later. Or you could simply talk to your team and let them know that while you prefer to send messages while they are top of mind, you do not expect a response outside work hours.

To start retraining your supervisor, start taking more time to respond, until you stretch it to a point where you do not respond outside work or between certain hours. Finally, if you feel up for it, you *can* have a conversation with your boss about communication processes. It may be more fruitful than you think. It's better for both you and your boss (not to mention the company) if you don't become an angry, resentful, silently fuming employee. I would normally encourage you to take the direct route first and talk about your concerns with your boss, but often with asshole bosses, you have to proceed carefully if you want to change things, and a respectful dialogue doesn't work as well for obvious reasons.

If you have issues like the above, and can't go to your boss, most companies have a process for handling complaints. There is often a hierarchy which you are probably familiar with: the first step is to address the issue with the person directly involved, then speak to your leader (or that person's leader.) Finally, if the issue is still unresolved, speak with Human Resources. Keep in mind that most workplaces take measures to protect themselves, politically and legally. You should, too. For that reason, document what you are doing, who you speak with, and what happens.

Watch and Learn

Take note of how the asshole works and manages, what they do badly and what they do well. Notice if you are not heard, understood, or respected inside difficult conversations. If nothing else this is a good learning opportunity, should you have interest in being in a leadership position and wish to avoid certain behaviors.

Realize too that not everyone will share your opinion of the asshole. That's because we have different experiences and perceptions of people, just as we have different backgrounds and ways of understanding others. For instance, sometimes assholes who are rude and condescending are viewed as being "decisive and driven," when really they are poor listeners who are closed-minded to others' thoughts and ideas.

Be Proactive

The flip side of what I said above, is that you, too, should cultivate relationships with people in higher levels in the organization. Relationships at every level are always beneficial. Who knows, once you've gained the respect and trust of the CEO, for instance, you may be asked to share your opinion of a certain manager.

Finally, take comfort that with time comes change. Change is the only constant in life. Sometimes if you stick it out in a company, the person will leave or move to another area. Likewise, you may get another offer or move within the organization.

I hear story after story of how someone's jerkish behavior catches up with them. Sometimes it's because they lose their temper and make inappropriate comments in front of witnesses, or harasses a subordinate who files a complaint.

You may not need to take any action; just keep your head down because over time, things change.

You also are a free person, of course. You can leave the company whenever you want. It's also much easier if you realize this is a valid option for you and you plan your exit. If you take another job, make sure when you research a company to find out about how they *actually* treat employees.

For example, what kinds of trainings do they offer? Do they seem to care about their employees beyond the value of their work? Do they have employees who have been there for awhile? Do they do any interpersonal employee training? These are things like team-building activities, leadership courses, specific skill-building trainings, and communication trainings...not just the basics, like customer service or sales training.

Zingerman's in Ann Arbor, Michigan is a great example of a company that does training well. In fact Zingerman's is renowned for its exemplary training practices, which led the company to create its own training division, ZingTrain.

Companies that spend money on training demonstrate they care about their employees' growth and view it as an investment. After all, we can all continue to learn and do better. The fact that an organization budgets for training is also a sign that the company is financially healthy enough to do so.

Providing training also shows that a company's leaders embody humility – meaning they know they can grow, learn, and change. Likewise, they recognize that employees want to grow and learn. Growth and learning is not viewed as a threat (i.e. if we educate her, she could leave); it's viewed as necessary and helpful. In today's ever-changing business climate, companies that value developing employees are more successful on every measure.

Finally, when you are evaluating new employers, notice a prospective company's mission. Do you believe in it? Does it mesh with your values? Does it seem authentic? Do they seem to deliver on this mission? Do they even have a mission? When you decide to work somewhere, it's not just you that benefits (job, money, growth, learning, etc.); employers benefit from having hired you, with all that you bring to the table.

Your Weaknesses

Switching jobs is a good time to consider your own weaknesses. We are told to focus on our strengths (and I do agree that it's important to use our strengths in whatever work we do.) But this is a good time also to give some thought to what you are terrible at and should probably not do – not only does that help keep you humble, it helps to find a job that fits your talents. Both you and your future employer will be better for it.

Take Time to Think

Finally, think about what you want in life. What is your personal work mission? What do you believe in? Who are you in the workplace? What kind of worker are you? Are you someone who prefers not to have to multi-task? Do you need different activities to do each day to keep your interest? Do you abhor constant interruptions? Are you an amazing problem-solver? Who are you at work?

Take a piece of paper and on the left column, make a list of things that drive you nuts. (But note that these should be significant items, not minor annoyances like a coworker clicking a pen repeatedly.) I'll share one of mine below to help get your thinking flowing.

After you have your list, make one in the right column, where next to each "deal breaker" (thing you hate), you list the *opposite*.

I'm having you do this because the things in the right column typically represent your core values. And depending on the length of your list, some of these will apply at work, while others may extend to your personal life.

For instance, if you absolutely hate when people interrupt you, know that being fully heard is a core value for you. If possible then, you may want to meet the people you will work with ahead of time to observe how they communicate.

Another example could be if you aren't skilled at keeping track of details, realize that you working in a job that requires heavy attention to detail is not setting yourself up for success.

One of my core values is best described as "nonverbal inclusion." Have you ever been part of a small group of people interacting and noticed that, as one person talks, he or she only makes eye contact with one other person, even though they are talking to four people, including you? Or people are turned slightly away so one person is left sitting just outside the group? I've noticed that in the latter situation, often the left-out person doesn't want to make waves so they suffer through the awkwardness, but don't feel connected to the rest of the group.

In small group interactions I like everyone to feel connected, so this is a core value of mine. I intentionally make eye contact with everyone, make sure we are all sitting in an inclusive manner, and I notice if someone seems to be feeling left out. If I notice someone seems to be left out, I first check my perceptions (after all, the person might be choosing to separate him or herself from the group.) If the exclusion isn't wanted, then I take steps to arrange seating or ask that person a question so they feel more included.

When people are left out intentionally or unintentionally, their voice may not be heard and they won't feel connected, which could lead to him or her not joining the group again. It could also mean that we miss out on some bit of wisdom, humor or insight that would only come from their mouth. (Yes, these are the kinds of things I spend time thinking about!)

Another example could be, if something you hate is a negative and gossipy work environment, you will want to be somewhere where the work environment and people are more positive (so definitely observe the environment in an office you are interviewing in!)

We all have preferences that are indicative of our core values - things like behavioral and communicative likes and dislikes. Figuring those out now can be valuable.

Uh-Oh, I'm the Asshole at Work - Fix It

If as you read this, you realize you can be the asshole there are things you can do right now to change this.

First, start showing interest in your employees' personal lives. Employees will have a more positive opinion of you and the organization when they feel they are actually cared about as a person. Don't pry – feel someone out for how much they seem comfortable sharing before you start asking them too many personal questions. When they open up to you, respond to *what they say* and resist the impulse to talk about yourself. For instance, if someone tells you their grandma just died, don't respond with a story about your grandma dying last year. Let it be about them – it's not your time to share.

If you don't feel like doing this or taking the time, sorry but it's not about how you feel. You can do the right thing simply because it is the right thing to do, and eventually, your feelings will adapt and support you. You will grow to care more.

Second, pay attention to what motivates some employees versus others. For example, some may like frequent verbal praise, while some may not care about that (or may even hate to be singled out), but instead may want a few free hours to attend their child's activities, grab a drink with a friend, or take their dog to the vet. Or they may want to work from home more. They may absolutely LOVE receiving public recognition – an award of some kind. They may prefer to get surprise bonuses. They may be happy with candy on their desk one morning. There's also nothing stopping you from asking what your employees really want.

Finally, and this is so important - <u>trust your employees to do their jobs</u>.

The Importance of Trust

One of the issues people who can be assholes have is that they don't trust their employees (or coworkers) and they ultimately do not respect them. It's difficult to force yourself to respect someone, but there is a pathway to respect – it's to trust that person. When you trust an employee and your trust is rewarded, then your respect automatically follows. The thing about trust is that to grow, it has to be exercised. You need to have faith in the people around you, which may not be easy for you at first. But you'll get there by practicing and exercising that trust.

To accomplish this start by looking for what they do well, and try not to notice their mistakes (at least the ones that won't harm the company or put anyone in danger.) Everybody makes mistakes, including you. No one needs to have them pointed out continuously. We all bloom when we are complimented and wilt when we are called out on mistakes or criticized too frequently.

Making mistakes can facilitate an employee's growth too, but not if they feel unappreciated in the first place. Then they will feel like a failure when mistakes are pointed out, and they will never see a mistake for the opportunity it can be - an opportunity for them to grow and learn.

You will probably have a hard time switching from distrust to trust. So first, start by proactively noticing what your employees do well and dwelling on those things.

When you go into work tomorrow, make it your mission to look for something done right – and comment on it. If you cannot find anything to comment on, look for something positive you can compliment – a new haircut, a good attitude, or a crisp shirt.

When you make this commenting a regular habit, eventually it will become easier to see the positive things. Trusting your employees will follow, as you will begin to care more about them. They will perform better too as they experience your trust in them. Your authentic respect for them will then grow naturally.

You should start to monitor employee engagement as well. Having your employees committed and engaged matters a lot.

The work you put into improving your behavior and communication will be worth it. Giving your personality a positive adjustment, or uncovering who you are capable of being, will ultimately make you, and everyone else around you, much happier. People prefer people who are nice to work with. Niceness, although maybe considered boring (or drama-free) by some, is extremely important.

You Can't Talk Yourself Out of Something You Behaved Yourself Into

Do realize that just because you have an epiphany or two and you change a few things doesn't mean that peoples' perceptions of you will change overnight. We have to *behave ourselves into* the person we really can be and continue being that person, before others notice and respond. And that takes effort, time, and patience. And more effort.

But it'll be worth it, and eventually it won't require so much effort. At some point, people around you will start to treat you better as well because they'll believe you've changed for the better.

Micro-Managing

If you find yourself micro-managing, then you are displaying a lack of trust of those under you. Let go of that need to control! It will help if you proactively integrate relaxation into your day. Take a hot tub soak on your lunch hour, do some yoga, deep breathing, pet your dog, watch a comedic video...figure out how to live in the present more often. Get hugs from those you love (hugs are proven to reduce anxiety.) When you're more relaxed, it will be easier for you to let go of the need to control others.

People who are micro-managed not only resent this, but they will also perform more poorly because of the scrutiny. Imagine that you are performing a task with someone looking over your shoulder, checking on you and directing you this or that way. Over time, happiness decreases. Resentment builds. Anger grows. You get the picture.

Employees like having a boss who believes in and trusts them, and in turn respects them. An asshole doesn't do these things.

People micro-manage for a variety of reasons. Some believe no one can do the job as well as they can. Some were raised in an environment where they had little to no control and now want to control everything around them as much as possible; this translates to hovering or being overly directive and controlling.

Maybe you are insecure about the position you hold, and you turn that insecurity toward others. (This is Psychology 101 – projection. If you constantly see faults or behaviors in others, it's often something that is in you.)

The thing to realize is that YOU ARE NOT HELPING. It IS possible to let go of the reins, and trust your employees, as I mentioned above. But it's understandable that it's hard at first – expect it to be. I want you to remember this point: the thing about trust is that it only grows through practicing it. You have to exercise trust to experience trusting others.

Eventually, once you've trusted someone and your trust is rewarded in less significant situations, then you will more easily extend trust in more important situations.

If You Manage Teams

If you manage teams, one of the critical characteristics to a high performing team is that they are united socially and task-wise. Competition between them may seem like a good way to motivate them, but it isn't. Your team will work best together if they are friends and care about each other, not if they are in competition with each other. They don't have to be best friends who hang out after work, but they should really care about each other. Caring about one another helps them have a group mentality versus a "me-first" mentality, which improves performance.

Bond Them

If you hired people specifically to work in a team, you can help ensure they will work well together in a myriad of ways. First, realize they expect to and should flourish in a team environment, otherwise they wouldn't have taken the job. You can increase the likelihood that they will work well together by sending them to a team retreat, to a conference together, or out for lunch on you.

There's also a lot they can learn as a team that will make them function better, and in return help them grow. Most employees love the opportunity to grow, especially when it's paid for by the company.

Teams will bend over backwards for their team members if they are united and truly work together, but if you don't give them time to develop relationships and continue to invest in those relationships they won't work as synergistically.

Synergy only happens through cohesion – not when you just throw a bunch of people together and call them a team, without doing the work required to really help them become a team. The examples of sending them to spend time offsite together are ways to help them bond socially, which creates cohesion.

The Importance of Follow-Up

It can be worthwhile to send employees to a conference or a fun team-building retreat. But temporary feel-good talks and highs can turn out to be pretty useless for the team, and to a company's bottom line, if there's no follow-up. For true change to occur, the employees must apply what they learn and a follow-up system should be in place. This not only helps your employees retain what they learned, it ensures that whoever you hired to facilitate the growth is committed for the length of time needed to make it happen.

A good trainer or coach will have a system in place for follow up, or a length of time they will work with you. This can be as simple as a feedback form (ideally you want more than this) or a series of check-in sessions by phone. Look for this follow-up if you want true change when you plan company trainings.

Speaking of coaches, as adults we don't have personal cheerleaders built into our lives. We may have a supportive spouse, but that's very different than someone giving us all their focus and being our life advocate in an intentional way. When we were children, we had our parents and teachers checking in with us, encouraging us to do better (hopefully), and giving us a nudge when needed. As adults we don't really have that. Simply having a coach to help hold us accountable to achieve our growth and goals can be huge. Why do you think personal and professional coaching is such a rapidly growing industry?

When and if you do hire someone to do a seminar, lead team activities, or serve as an ongoing coaching resource to your employees, make sure that person stays long enough for your employees to experience true positive change.

Doing all of these things takes planning, time, and effort, but it is well worth it. It is also much cheaper ultimately than disgruntled employees who will call in more often, tear down the work environment, sue, and eventually cost you in turnover.

Workplace Takeaways

If you are the difficult person, put into practice what you've learned here. Pick some things and start doing them tomorrow (or tonight!) I also strongly suggest hiring a coach to help you get a realistic view of yourself and how you can improve.

If you work for a person who is difficult, start thinking about what you are able to do and change, as well as what you should and should not do going forward.

If you hired that difficult person, begin implementing changes required for them to start engaging and empowering their employees. Hire a coach for them. Some people just do not have the skills or self-awareness to improve their communication and would benefit from a trained third party's help.

And if you are the employee who is stuck, take heart. If the asshole near you doesn't leave or get fired, other doors will open for you at the right time. Don't give up.

Final Thoughts

We all have at least one asshole in our lives. The asshole may be in our family, at our work, or in our bed. But there's so much we can do to become better, happier, and more fulfilled. And if the asshole is you, the same applies. You can become a better, happier and more fulfilled version of yourself.

Don't let reading this book become a momentary feel-good emotional boost that you then forget about. Get out there and try out what you've learned!

Reviews

If you found value in this book, please place a review on its Amazon page. Authentic reviews help other readers discover this book, they help me, and they are **much** appreciated!

If you'd prefer to send me a more personalized review, get in touch by visiting my business page, www.optimizingrelationships.com.

You can also find me on Instagram (sarahbrabbsassholebook), on facebook.com/optimizingrelationships, and on twitter @sarahlbrabbs.

Made in the USA
San Bernardino, CA
11 November 2019

59721009R00053